What a b

with trams clanging, and ... ng o'er the sets.
Horse drawn wagons drawn up by the sea,
And on the corner, bookies runners, taking bets.

The sounds of ship-building came from the yards,
That lined the Camber with their slips.
Craftsmen on board the vessels moored to bollards,
Drilling and hammering, working on the ships.

Overhead cranes of "Fraser & Whites",
travelling to and fro, unloading the colliers,
Down in the hold, the grab takes it's bites.
Coal for home fires, and to stoke the boilers.

Dining rooms in the street, clean and tidy,
Ready to feed the workers at mid-day.
To restore their energy and nourish the body,
With mugs of hot tea, that's the old Pompey way.

The Cathedral clock looks down, on the scene below,
At its parishioners going about their daily toil.
The landmark of the High Street stands on show,
It has seen them all, from commoner to royal.

The Garrison Church, stood, in all its glory,
And still stands, despite the ravages of war.
Soldiers from many regiments, shared in its story,
And brave men left, to return no more.

F. Ford

THE CAMBER : FRASER & WHITE

The Urchin

Down to the Camber my Ma sent me,
to give her a rest no doubt,
With bread and dipping and a bottle of cold tea.
"Now behave yourself, or you will get a clout".
With this warning ringing in my ears
I set off with fishing line and bait.
Then I sat there, for what seemed like years.
"Ahoy there, any luck yet mate?"
A passing skipper gives me a shout.
"No, only a couple of baby crabs guv'nor.
For there ain't no fish here about."
"Catch this then sonny, here's your supper"
And a plaice landed at my feet.
Quick as a flash I thanked the man.
Now I could give my Ma a tasty treat.
Thoughts of her cooking came as I ran.
Then home at last puffed out and weary
I held the fish up for her to see.
"My what a whopper" she said so merry.
Quickly I explained that it was given to me.
"Never mind your patience was rewarded"
and as a smile played around her lips
"We'll have it tonight, nicely filleted,
with four penn'eth of salty chips."

F. Ford

Streets and their History

The area we call Old Portsmouth grew up around one of the oldest settlements on the Island Of Portsea. The principal reason for the settlement seems to have been the Camber where ships could dock and be repaired. By the 1190s the area was sufficiently built up for a wealthy merchant John De Gisors to provide the land for the church to be built on. The general history of the area and the church has been covered by many books over the years and we will not attempt to repeat them. This booklet uses our normal theme of memories of what life was like in the area in the twenties and thirties.

Bath Square

Named after the baths of the Quebec Hotel.

The Still & West Country House

First listed in the trade directories in 1784 as the Still. The & West Country House part of the name was added when it combined with East & West Country House another pub that was in Bath Square. It is best remembered as a Gales house.

Customs Watch House

"Opposite Uncle's was the Custom's Hailing station. This establishment entered my life in a practical way much later, in 1945 to be precise, when I returned from the Far East as No.1 of a corvette to pay off. The Custom Officer who came to clear us was old, and had obviously been dug out for war service. When he discovered I was the son of one of 'those Kemp girls' he stretched Custom Regulations to breaking point. I was afraid to ask him the basis of his dreamy look when I told him my mother's name but maybe they have both resolved it on a higher plane."

Pickfords, general carriers

Were at Quebec House, a wooden house that was erected in 1754 as the baths for the nearby Quebec Hotel. The street takes its name from the baths.

"Alongside the Hailing Station was Pickford's warehouse with its jetty where the coasters from the Isle of

Wight unloaded. These coasters were about 150 feet long as I remember, and were driven by a single cylinder diesel engine called a Kromhout. It was a two stroke with a deep booming exhaust and seemed to fire about once a minute. The engine had to be stopped and restarted in order to go astern and apparently the restarting was rather uncertain. The skipper must have had a few bad moments, but if he timed his arrival to coincide with the ebb tide which rushes round this jetty, his problem would be going against it rather than worries about going astern. I never knew what cargo the Pickford boats landed but I well recall that the goods were loaded onto Foden wagons which had a fascinating chain-driven final drive to the rear wheels. All these mechanical details were fully exposed of course, the tyres were solid rubber. Between Pickfords and the Hailing Station there was a tiny pier which we called 'The Skids'. You could catch fair sized crabs by dangling a second-hand fish head on a piece of string in the rather murky waters at this point. Maybe they just needed to come up for air."

1 Coal Exchange

First listed in the trade directories in 1830 when it was known as the North Country, by 1847 it had become the Jolly Sailor and Coal Exchange, by 1859 the Jolly Sailor part of the name had been dropped. Its name reflects the trade with the north of the country in coal. It has recently been extensively modernised and combined with the adjacent Union Tavern reopening as the Spice Island Inn.

3 W. Moody, fish salesman

5 G. Cook, fish salesmen

11 C. Frampton, fish salesman

Broad Street

West side

1 D. A. P. Grogan, boat proprietor

3 T. Cobbett, photographer

7 G. Feltham & Sons, boat builders

here is West Street

13 The Seagull

Rebuilt in 1900 as a Brickwood's pub and has been attributed to various local architects. It closed as a pub as reopened as a restaurant in 1971.

15 W. Clark, shopkeeper

17 Mrs E. Theobald, shopkeeper

"Opposite the other road to the quay was 'our' sweet shop owned by an Italian family called by us Patracker, I suggest the name was probably Patraccia (Petracca - Ed) but I do remember that they did a remarkably good ice cream cornet for a half-penny. It was incongruous that there was another sweet shop next door but one, run by a couple called Clark. Their sherbet dabs were marginally better so, presumably, both shops prospered."

27A Harry. J. Feltham, boat builder

31 G. Zammit, shopkeeper

33 Mrs. M. Liddiard, shopkeeper

here is Bathing Lane

35 J. Dryden, wardrobe dealer

39 T. Wooten later W. Hogg, dining rooms

53 Fortitude Tavern.

Built in around 1786, it is first listed in the trade directories in 1823. The sign was repainted a few years ago. Last listed as a pub in 1923.

55 G. Cook, fish salesman

here is Rowe's Alley

57 J. Petracca, hair dresser

59-61 later Reflex Photo Works Ltd.

65 Union Tavern

First listed in the trade directories in 1823 although there was a Union at Point in 1716.

Here was the Floating Bridge Ferry to Gosport

"Broad Street always seemed full of vehicles. On one side of the street a queue of cars and vans waited for the Isle Of Wight car ferry. Whilst on the other side a line of horse drawn wagons waited for the Gosport car ferry, which clawed its way across the harbour at half hour intervals pulling itself across on massive chains. When the tide was low the slope down to the ferry became steeper and seaweed was also uncovered making negotiating it perilous. I saw one horse lose its footing and with the weight of the wagon pushing it the poor horse missed the ramp and slid into the sea. All the drivers rushed to the rescue and eventually freed the animal from the shafts and led it back up the road where it stood shaking like a leaf. A cover was put on its back and the driver spoke to it in a soft voice to pacify it. The drivers of these horses really cared for them for I have seen them unhitch their horse and use it to assist another horse and cart to leave the ferry when the slope was so sheer. What with the two queues of traffic waiting to board the ferries and the trams at the terminus at Point there was not a lot of street left."

"The floating bridge pulled itself across to Gosport on massive chains anchored each end to huge weights sunk in wells which were always full of rainwater. A foot passenger could cross for one penny unless one of the crew was either a relation or friend when it was much cheaper! Alongside was the slipway where the Isle of Wight cattle and vehicle ferries came in. Originally the boats were lighters, towed and manoeuvred by a steam tug which landed the vehicle traffic over a portable ramp. There were a few cars and a very occasional horse and cart but the red letter day each week was Thursday or 'Cattle Ferry' day. On this day the ferry was loaded with bullocks, sheep and pigs. After they landed they were driven up Broad Street, presumably to meet a sticky end.

"POINT"

We children provided ourselves with sticks for Cattle Thursday, but I can never recall any one of us having the courage to approach closely enough to actually use them. Occasionally a pig would make a bid for freedom by falling into the sea. Folklore maintained that if a pig swam it would cut its own throat with its front trotters. Consequently, since all children are naturally morbid, we used to watch these aquatic pigs with great excitement but they were always recovered with their throats intact."

East Side

2 Vosper & Co. Ltd. Ship builders

4 G. Feltham & Sons, boat builders

"Further down on the same side as the Blue Posts was the home of an old Pointer called Sid Leverett. He owned the 'Round the Harbour' boats which plied from Southsea beach and his imposing house had a railed enclosure on the roof. Rumour had it that Sid stood on the roof with a telescope to see that the number of passengers in his boats tallied with the receipts. This was almost certainly apocryphal, but I can remember my Aunty Flo advising me to be very polite to Mr Leverett in case he might leave me something in his will. Unless Mr Leverett is still alive (and if he is he must be a centenarian) my aunt's hopes were groundless. I believe there is a seat dedicated to Sid on the Point and I believe he was, at one time, the chairman of the Portsmouth Football Club."

here is Dore's Court

38 Old Blue Posts.

An old coaching inn built in 1613. It burnt down in 1870 and was rebuilt. This version was short lived as it was bombed.

"Down the street past Vospers was the Old Blue Posts, a naval pub with a very long history. The landlord was my Uncle Fred Bowman and my Aunty Flo, yet another Kemp. Whether they were the last landlords before it was demolished by a German bomb I am not certain (no -Ed). I remember meeting a variety of young naval officers at the Blue Posts including a Crown Prince of Siam who was a midshipman in the Royal Navy. My uncle was a retired Engineer Officer who had risen to commissioned rank from being an artificer. I believe he was a Lt. Cmmdr(E) on retirement and that Brickwoods made a practise of appointing ex-naval tenants to this historic pub which had been a coaching house in the past. One would often meet sprigs of foreign royalty in my uncle's pub since it was common for foreign royalties to give their offspring a taste of the rigours of the British Navy."

40 Vosper & Co. Ltd., motor garage
42-46 W. G. Lucas & Son, sail makers
48-50 A. W. Clemens, boat builder
54 G. Haywood, tobacconist
56 Shell-Mex Ltd was earlier the Black Swan
62 The Becket Club Room
68 P. Kemp, shopkeeper
70 Miss K. Blackman, draper
here is East Street
72 L. Green, confectioner
74 A. Fogwill, boot and shoe maker
78 Timothy White Ltd., hardware stores
82-84 Crouchers Ltd., removals and storage
86 R. Goring, general dealer
92 Somerset Tavern.

First listed as King's Head in 1716 it became the Somerset by 1874. It later became the Somerset Cafe.

98 Mrs. S. Grogan, dining rooms

"A little down the street from No.27 an old lady called gran Grogan lived. One of my sisters told me she was a witch and I was scared to pass her house. Eventually I did meet the lady and found she was charming and quite un-witch like. I believe her descendants now run the restaurant at the ferry terminal"

100 Star & Garter.

First listed in 1784 it survived until the war when it suffered bomb damage. It was demolished in 1954.

Southern Railway Company Steam Packet Service

Crown Street formerly Coach And Horses Street.

The Hampshire Metal Co. Ltd., wholesale rag, metal and skin merchants

1-3 W. Smith, iron and metal merchant

East Street was earlier known as Smock Alley.

East Side

16 Shovellers' Arms.

First listed as the Three Tuns in 1784, becoming the Shovellers Arms after 1898. It closed in 1928.

A. Burnett & Sons, contractors

22 Portsea Island Mutual Co-operative Society Ltd., coal stores

Fraser & White Ltd., coal stores

"The Camber or the Quay as we called it was a fascinating other world to the Pointer children. It was dominated by a coal firm called Fraser and White who built most impressive silos for their coal and unloaded the coasters with an electrically operated gantry. The massive grab lifted several tons of coal each time and then dumped it out of sight behind the concrete wall with a satisfying crash. The Pointers used to arm themselves with buckets and remove slack which was the local name for small coal. As there never seemed to be any secrecy about this activity, I can only assume that Fraser and White had no objections."

"In winter I approached the Camber from the 'Black Side', the side where the collier boats unloaded their coal via overhead cranes, taking the coal from their holds and depositing it into the large hoppers behind thehigh concrete wall of the coal-yard. This was owned by a firm called Fraser & Whites. My father who drove a coal cart in the winter took me with him on Saturdays to collect a load of coal from the camber. We were weighed with an empty cart on arrival and weighed again with a full load on leaving the yard. To get the coal the horse and cart was backed up to the hopper, our empty bag held on a pair of scales and the hopper opened to fill the one cwt bag. Holding these bags up was hard work for

CAMBER BRIDGE

me and usually resulted in losing some skin off my knuckles, and on a wet day it was far from pleasant. I looked forward to a mug of hot tea from Grogan's cafe in Broad Street when we had finished. The horse would have his nose bag on whilst we were there, then it was off to do our rounds."

54 Bridge Tavern.

First listed in 1863, the site is mentioned in a lease of 1656 from the Corporation to a brewery for 1,000 years at a rent of 12d and two fat capons a year.

West Side

J. Birkett, motor boat proprietor

here is Cromwell Terrace this consisted of small tenements that were only twelve feet deep and ten feet wide.

21 The Anchor, first listed in 1874.

23 Fraser & White Ltd., offices

27 Camber House, first listed in 1863 it closed in 1937.

High Street

South-East side

Portsmouth Grammar School housed in buildings that at an earlier date where the Cambridge Barracks

10 Bramsdon & Childs, solicitors.

More infamous in earlier times as this was where the Duke Of Buckingham was murdered.

11 A. Ford, architect

17 L. Bartlett, motor engineer

21 Crown Bedding Co. Ltd.

here is Barrack Street

26 London Joint City & Midland Bank Ltd.

30 The George Hotel

Known from 1693 to 1716 as the Wagon and Lamb, it had become the George Hotel by 1805 when Nelson is reputed to have spent his last time ashore before leaving for Trafalgar. It was one of the old coaching inns of the town and like many other buildings was bombed in 1941.

GUILDHALL HALL/MUSEUM

33 Lloyds Bank Ltd.
35 Cousins & Burbidge, solicitors
37-38 Smith & Vosper Ltd, grocers
here is Pembroke Road
39 W. Dod, antique dealer
40 T. Cook & Co., fishmongers
41 Dolphin Family & Commercial Hotel

First listed in 1716. It was extremely lucky to survive the war as buildings all around it were badly damaged.

42 Borough of Portsmouth Museum. This was housed in the old Townhall that had been built in 1837 and was replaced by the new townhall in 1890.

44-45 C. M. Elliot, physician and surgeon
46 Charpentier Ltd, stationers
47 Gale & Son, butchers
48 Snook & Sons Ltd., egg merchants
49 Silvertown, India Rubber, Gutta Percha & Telegraph Works Co. Ltd.
49 Palmer Tyre Ltd., cycle tyre makers
52 Jepps & Co., general furnishers
54 Moncks Oyster Depot
55-56 Y.M.C.A.

Was formerly the Fountain Inn from 1768 until 1874 when it became The Soldiers Hostel run by Miss Sarah Robinson. This was a similar establishment to the later Sailors' Rests. It was demolished in 1970 and replaced by flats.

58 Jepps & Co., invalid furniture makers
here is Grand Parade
York & Pier Hotel

First listed as the Antelope from 1830, becoming York & Pier Hotel by 1859 it became yet another war time casualty

62 Wellington Hotel

First listed in 1823 as the Duke of Wellington becoming the Wellington Hotel by 1863.

63 G. Tullet, shopkeeper
here is Battery Row

North-West Side

65 Quinto Cecconi & Son, musical instrument makers

"The last port of call on this orgy of nostalgia is at a little shop at the extreme end of Broad Street opposite Sallyport. This was a musical instrument workshop run by yet more Italians called Giacconi (Cecconi -Ed). They repaired wind and percussion instruments for the Marine bandstand. Their dusty windows contained examples of military instruments of the past. There was a serpent, keyed bugles, early natural horns and two key horns, very early cornets and bugles and some early rope tensioned side drums. I must have shown a most precocious interest to the Giacconi brothers because they allowed me to blow these antiques albeit not very musically. I particularly remember them beating out dents in a pair of timpani which they assured me had been damaged aboard a ship in heavy weather."

67 Bell Tavern

First listed in 1784 as the Bell sometime after 1923 it became a house.

"We moved into the ground floor flat of what had once been a public-house called, I believe, the Bell Tavern. It consisted of three largish rooms, outside toilet and a coal-house but no bathroom. Mrs. Thompson, wife of an Admiralty tug-skipper, was the landlady and occupied a more prestigious first-floor flat. Access to their accommodation was by a quaint spiral stairway which carried up to the top floor flat occupied by the Pearce's, a naval Petty Officer and his family. All the flats had electric lighting, gas cookers and coal fires, facilities which were not enjoyed by all who lived in Old Portsmouth in those days. In the cellars beneath our flat the redundant barrel trestles were still in place, used now for the storage of old furniture and similar junk together with the upper flat's coal. Initially, I thought the cellars a great place to explore but after hearing, or imagining, the scurry of rats in odd corners I became less enthusiastic about entering the cellars to put coins in the meters down there. On several occasions, at the height of the spring tides the cellars flooded nearly up to street level. Whether this was due to the rising water-table or from flood water draining down through the drayman's hatchway I am not sure. Suffice to say that access to the meters was hazardous, if adventurous, and the electrics must have been highly suspect by today's standards."

68 A. Russell, fried fish shop
69 D & E Knight, dining rooms
70 Mrs. E Cottrell, confectioner
71 D. Myers, tailor
74 Spencer & Co, opticians
77 G. Robinson, bookbinder
83 Mew Langton & Co. Ltd., wine & spirit merchants
here is Oyster Street
84 Mrs F. Souter, grocer
85 G. Souter, ironmonger
87 Post Office
88 A. Scott, confectioner
89 C. Lillington, boot maker
91 Mrs Isaacs, fruiterer
92 P. Jose, tailor
93 Abrahams & Sons, watchmakers
here is Church Lane
Cathedral Church of St Thomas of Canterbury.

Many books have been written which give a full account of the church's history. The church was first consecrated in 1188 having been built on a site given by the wealthy merchant John De Gisors. It was completed in 1196 and hallowed. The parish was separated from St Mary's in 1320. It was restored in 1691 after Civil War damage when the tower was rebuilt at the West End. The next major changes were made in the thirties when the new nave was added along with two aisles. Finally the temporary wall that was erected then was removed and the new west end completed in 1991.

96 A. Freeman & Co., hairdresser
97 Ye Olde Towne Tea Rooms
98 A. Allan, butcher

99 Madame Ald, ladies' outfitter
101 Christian Science Reading Rooms
102 Bentall & Trayler Ltd., hosiers
here is Lombard Street
103 Trayler & Co., military outfitters
104 T. Main, ironmonger and cycle agent
105 National Sailors' & Firemen's Union
106 J. Williams & Co., ship chandlers
107 J. Phillips, boot maker
108 A. J. Barrett Ltd, chemists
109 Provincial Grand Lodge Masonic Office
110 Phoenix Masonic Lodge
111 Borough Of Portsmouth Electricity Office
112 W. H. Barrell Ltd., lithographers
114-116 W. H. Barrell Ltd., printers
117 B. West, hairdresser
118 A. Greaves, boot maker
119 Duke of Buckingham

Known from 1784 until 1851 as the Green Dragon. It had become the Cambridge Tavern by 1859 and the Duke of Buckingham by 1900. The house was rebuilt in 1968/9 and refronted in 1991.

here is Highbury Street
120 W. Long, bookseller
122 A. Whittman, tobacconist
123 J. Woodhouse & Son, military outfitters
124 Hobbs & Brutton, solicitors
126 Provincial Tramways Garage
Unitarian Church

In 1718 a Presbyterian Chapel was built on the site of William Mudge's Malthouse. The congregation became Unitarian. Hymns were accompanied in the early days by a string group as in the church records we are told of the installation of the organ in 1846 and subsequent disposal of the instruments. With various alterations over the years it survived until 1941 when it was bombed. The new church known as the John Pounds Memorial Church was built in 1955/56. The foundation stone was laid by Sir Adrian Boult. John Pounds is buried in the churchyard.

127 J. Jestico, cabinet maker
129 G. Clark, solicitor
132 Hellard & Bechervaise, solicitors
132½ Houston & Blake, dental surgeons
135 J. Nicholson, refreshment rooms
136 J. Bloxham, boot maker
137 E. Sykes, tobacconist
138 Miss Bore, shopkeeper
139 W. Bulford, watchmaker
140 W. Lambert, fried fish shop
141 Prince Consort

Named in the trade directory of 1887 otherwise only listed as a beer retailer from 1863 until 1940

142 W. Cooper, fried fish shop
143 R. Hewitt, greengrocer
144 Magdala Arms

Named in the trade directory of 1887 otherwise listed as a beer retailer from 1863 until 1934.

146 J. Hargreaves, athletic outfitters
147 Mrs. Hargreaves, confectioner
148 Biscoe-Smith & Blagg, solicitors

Highbury Street was earlier St Mary's Street named after St Mary's Chapel of Ease. It takes its later name from Highbury Congregational Chapel.

"This was quite narrow and full of old houses and shops. It was originally much longer but the power station was built on part off the site. The houses where all different styles and heights."

East Side

2 Angel & County Court Tavern

Known from 1716 to 1851 as the White Horse, it became the Angel by 1859 and the Angel & County Court Tavern by 1865.

here is St Thomas Street
16 Beer Retailer
18 Beer Retailer
20 H. Marchment, butcher
here is Warblington Street
22 Cross Keys Tavern

First listed in 1859 when the street was St Mary's Street.

24 J. Saunders, greengrocer
26 Mrs. S. Beech, pork butcher

"This building was quite old probably 18th century and the shop front had a huge bay."

30 A. Locock, grocer
34 Mrs. E. Stockwell, fancy draper
42 W. Smith, bottle merchant
44 Mrs. E. Nash, shopkeeper
46 Mrs. R. Clancey, shopkeeper
54 Mrs. L. Patterson, greengrocer
here is Amoury Lane
60 Portsmouth Electrical Fittings Co.
66 Highbury Engineering Co.
76 Beer Retailer
78 John Pounds House

A small wooden fronted house where John Pounds founded his Ragged School in his cobblers shop. It was taken down for safe keeping in the war and the timbers rotted.

84 J. George, umbrella repairer

West side
5-7 Wootton Trading Co. Ltd. And Thomas Allen, carriers
Portsmouth Almshouses
Masonic Hall
here is King Street
13 J. Saunders, coal dealer
here is Crown Street

King Street

North East Side

T Barnes, iron and metal merchant

Phoenix Tavern - first mentioned as the Phoenix on a lease dated 1774, it was earlier known as the Shipwrights Arms.

P. Rice, government stores

South West Side

Portsmouth Bonding Stores Ltd.

> "There were about eleven or twelve of them. These buildings had heavy wooden arched doors rising from the pavement. This was to allow the goods to be put into the buildings with the least difficulty."
>
> At the end of the street the Quay Gate used to stand which led to the bridge across the Camber.

Lombard Street the portion by St Thomas' Church was earlier called Golden Lion Lane, it was widened in 1869 at a cost of £3,000 to £4,000.

East Side

4 M. Coltherup, builder

6 W. Hatton, hair dresser

here is St Thomas's Street

Fraser & White Ltd., coal merchants

28 G. Bishop, wine merchant

34 Union Petroleum Products Co. Ltd.

West Side

1 The Ruby

Listed in trade directories from 1851 to 1923

19 G. Kent, ships' chandler

37 T. Warne, tailor

LOMBARD STREET

Nobbs Lane

"This small alley housed about ten houses and what was I suppose for ordinary folk at that period reasonable accommodation, with three rooms one on top of the other. Very poor sanitation and water supply."

R. Wood & Son, brass founders & finishers

Oyster Street

West Side

5 White Hart

First listed in the 1784 trade directory.

7 W. Giles, fruiterer

17 Victoria Chambers, lodging house

here is White Hart Alley

19 H. Whymark, shopkeeper

23 Beer Retailer

37 J. Moore, sheet metal worker

43-45 Beer Retailer

East Side

36 F. Thatcher, motor engineer

40 King & Queen Tavern

First listed in the 1784 trade directory

46 A. J. Bishop, cooper

48 A. Whymark, lodging house

54 C. White, tobacconist

56 W. White, lodging house

58 American Hotel

First listed as the Shipwrights Arms in 1784, by 1859 it had become the Forfarshore Tavern and by 1887 the American Hotel.

PEMBROKE ROAD

Pembroke Road, was earlier Fighting Cock Lane presumably after the public house that used to be in the street. Before that it was Genmell Street for which no explanation has been found.

North Side

1 Brooklands Dairy (H. R. White & Co. Ltd.)

3 Albert Gardner, picture frame makers, fine art dealers

5 The Cement Supply Co. Ltd.

9 Miss Annie Walters, greengrocers

11 Charpentier Ltd., typewriter stores

here is Penny Street

19 Pembroke House

21 Cole & Son, gun makers

23 Royal Naval Club

here is St Nicholas Street

First Church of Christ Scientist

There has been a church on this site for many years. In 1810 the Wesleyans built a new church on a former Quaker site. It was a very large church that could seat 2,000 and had a white brick front. It was modernised in 1889 but by 1919 financial problems led to its closure. It was sold to the Baptists but they soon resold the building to the Christian Scientists. Like many other buildings in the area it became a war time casualty.

33 Royal Swan

First listed in the trade directories in 1784.

Portsmouth & Southern Counties Eye & Ear Hospital

here is Clarence View

Clarence & Victoria Barracks

South Side

2 Mrs H. Besant, wardrobe dealer

4-6 Mrs E. James, tobacconist

6 Miss Ivy James, School of Dancing

10 Albert Higgins, tobacconist

12 Portsmouth Charity Organisation Society

14 Boy Scouts Association

16 William Dod, antique dealer

18 Arthur Taylor, watch maker
20 The Pembroke

Listed in the trade directories from 1823 to 1875 as the Blue Post. In 1887 it was the Little Blue Posts and by 1898 had taken its present name

here is Penny Street
Royal Garrison Church Room

St Nicholas Street

West Side
Green Row Rooms
E. Wild, garage

East Side
The Garrison Racquet Court
First Church of Christ Scientist Sunday School

St Thomas's Street

South East Side
9-10 J. Barnes, dealer in old government stores
15 Beer Retailer
here is Hampton Court
Baptist Church

Meetings were first held in a cottage on the site in 1640. The chapel was built in 1693. In 1798 after a dispute the Trinitarian Baptists moved to Clarence Street while the Unitarian Baptists remained here. In 1864 it was enlarged the old chapel forming the chancel of the new church. Like the nearby Unitarian Church in the High Street it survived until the war. After the war the members united with the High Street church.

here is Highbury Street
34 C. Branton, boot maker.

"On the corner of Highbury Street and St Thomas's Street stood the thatched house of the bootmaker"

38-39 W. H. Barrell Ltd., stationers, works

ST THOMAS' STREET

40 J. Loney, apartments
44 Gieves Ltd., baggage stores
52 St Thomas Arms

In the 1887 trade directory otherwise listed as beer retailer from 1874 to 1923.

here is Lombard Street
here is Church Lane
55 A. Baxter, general smith
56 A. Twyman, coal merchants
Old Blue Bell

First listed in the 1716 when it is described as being in Oyster Street and named the Bell, by 1823 it was known as the Old Blue Bell.

North West Side
59 W. Way, grocer
here is Lombard Street
72 H. Morris, fried fish shop
82 Vice-Consul for Finland
82 Vice-Consul for Russia
Court House
88 Wise Time Co. Ltd., clockmakers
here is Highbury Street
89 The Stag

First listed in the 1863 trade directory.

97 W. Daniels, Soda manufacturers
98 Mrs. Saunders, greengrocers
here is Vicarage Court
100-102 H. Pert & Sons, coach builders & wheelwrights
103 A. Bevis, builder
The Portsmouth Brewery, bonded stores
here is St Thomas's Court this had three small houses in 1901.
here is Nobbs Lane
111 J & W Cottrell, motor boat proprietors
112 A. Williams, cabinet maker
Military Police Quarters

Warblington Street reputedly named after Warblington Castle from which the bricks where taken for the houses. It was earlier known by various versions of Hogmarket Street.

South Side

2-3 Colewort Arms Hotel

First listed in 1716 as the London 'Prentice, later it was the Albert, then the Grapes. By 1887 it was the Colewort Arms.

7 W. Weston, shopkeeper

8 J. Cooper, fried fish shop

here is Fleets Court

here is Nobbs Lane

11 J. Malley, general merchant

here is Buckler's Court

15 R. Buckler, grocer

19 The Lord Clyde

Listed as the Military Arms in 1865 by 1887 it had become the Lord Clyde.

Price's Bakery

here is Aylott's Court

28 A. Burnett & Sons, carriers

29 J. Cooley, fried fish shop

North Side

33 Beehive Tap

The tap of the Beehive brewery first listed in the 1847 trade directory.

here is St George's Place

39 The Prince Of Wales

Listed as the Prince of Wales from 1865 to 1887, becoming the Mafeking by 1927, otherwise listed as beer retailer until 1958.

45 T. Barnes, smith

Warblington Street Mission Hall & Institute

General Memories of the Area

"In the twenties and thirties Old Portsmouth, as it is still affectionately known, was an area of grandiose, with the imposing architecture of the buildings on each side of the High Street. The Cathedral Church of St. Thomas of Canterbury being the centre of attraction standing head and shoulders above the surrounding cluster of historic houses. I'm reminded of that old metaphor "If these walls could only speak, what tales they could tell".

My memories of this part of Portsmouth really start with the presentation of a book given to me by the school on the occasion of King George V and Queen Mary's silver jubilee. This little blue book contained facets of Old Portsmouth that started me off dreaming of Old Portsmouth as it was. I wandered along the High Street observing, with the help of my little blue book, objects that I had given scant interest in before. And even as a boy I was too shy to enter the old Guildhall which was the City Museum. I could never find anyone else to accompany me into that splendid building. I can see it now in my minds eye, its frontage of four columns carrying a cornice and pediment. The Cathedral was another building which I was shy of entering.

As I stood in the High Street my young mind would fantasise on what days gone by could have been like. Of seeing the press gang striding along looking for likely victims to be pressed into the King's Navy, and of seeing these men fleeing up the side streets and hiding in the tunnels that I had been told criss crossed the old town in those days. I could well imagine the ladies of yore descending from their carriages, gathering their voluminous skirts around them and sweeping through the extra wide front doors, no doubt especially built to accommodate such fashions. And if I happened to be nearby as the grand lady passed, I would have behaved like a little gentleman and touch my hat to her with due respect and decorum, a little of which would not go amiss today.

The clanging of a passing tram jolted me out of my day dreams and bought me back to reality. I remember looking for the house in which the Duke of Buckingham was done to death. I had been told that you could still see the blood on one of the windows, so I paid special attention to those. Although I examined the glass with a scrutiny that would have done justice to Sherlock Holmes, I did not discern any such mark whatsoever.

One thing that I did discover at that time, was that the house numbers ran down one side and back on the other. I felt pleased that I had observed something that was not mentioned in my little blue book.

I think High Street made an impression on me because I lived in a district that had row upon row of terraced houses, so much uniformity. Old Portsmouth was so different with almost each building present in its own style of facade.

I can remember looking in the window of Charpentier's the printers at the various publications that were on display. Such as bus and railway timetables, illustrated guides, stationery, etc. and I also noticed they carried a Royal Warrant. That day I also looked for and found John Pound's cobblers shop in Highbury Street. I remember touching the door frame and wondering perhaps I had touched a spot that the famous cobbler had actually touched. Just to increase the chance I patted a few more places. As the book informed me that his grave was in the grounds of the Unitarian Chapel in the High Street I made that my next port of call.

Eventually I found myself by Sallyport and I remember the little house that stood alongside it. I was now in the part of Old Portsmouth that was, and is still by some, called Spice Island. Point Barracks was enclosed by a high wall in those days and I was more familiar with Spice Island having spent some of my time fishing in the Camber. Broad Street always seemed to me to be so much busier than High Street with a general air of hustle and bustle hanging over the place. What with the trams rattling along to the terminus at Point and shunting over to the other track, waiting for the next tram to take its place. The line of traffic, mostly horse drawn wagons queuing for the Gosport chain ferry and the traffic on the other side waiting for the Isle of Wight car ferry. Then there were the coal carts coming and going, collecting their loads of coal from the Camber, their steel tyres rumbling over the granite sets. The call of the drivers to their horses "Whoa there" as they came to a halt or with a click of their tongue "Get on then" to move off again.

Vosper's shipyard also added to the general hubbub of noise with the sounds of shipwrights busy at their trade. I remember peering through the open door of one of the smaller boat yards and watching yachts being built, surrounded by wooden scaffolding. I could only see the underside of course, I'd no idea what the topside looked like. The smell of the timbers drifted under my nose, a lovely clean aroma of teak, spruce and elm, Spice Island indeed, I thought.

I still like to visit Old Portsmouth and sit at Point and remember my early days, but all the above times are gone, more the pity."

F. Ford

"I was born in London on the 9th of December 1921. My father, Albert Williams was born in Copnor and my mother, Ida Rose, (nee Kemp) was born at 27 Broad Street, Point. My paternal grandfather, Frederick Williams started work as a farm labourer. He only went to school on one occasion, the family story being that, since he entered school at the advanced age of eight he was put in Standard One among the infants. Since he was large (he ultimately grew to 6' 3") the infant furniture was not designed for his bulk and on the first occasion he tried to get out of his chair, the horseshoe shaped top came with him. He couldn't take the laughter and never returned. In consequence he was illiterate despite being one of the most intelligent men I have ever known. He was a superb singer and was an accomplished player on the concertina. He taught me many songs of his youth and some of them still feature in the ballad recitals I give occasionally. He later became a Dockyard labourer and told me the pitiful story of his promotion to foreman. This advancement lasted exactly one week. One of his duties in his new position was to make out the time sheets for his men. It was then that his illiteracy was revealed and he was forced to take demotion.

My mother came from a more genteel background. Her father was an importer of cork, (he apparently carried out this business at 27 Broad Street) and my mother was a 'governess'. She was, in fact, headmistress of a tiny school but the older word was always used in the family.

My grandfather, who was known as 'Pamp' owned an ornate American reed organ which he played beautifully. Apparently he was also a reserve organist for St. Thomas's Church (now Portsmouth Cathedral). All my cousins sang in the church choir and both my sisters and I have always been competent singers. I remember my amazement when I first went to prep school, to find that there were actually children who could not sing! I seem to remember that all Pointers could sing, especially the late night customers at the Still and West. My grandmother's school was in Broad Street and was opposite 27 Broad Street. By the time I entered the

'Point' scene it was little more than a derelict hut, but my sister Dorothy and her cousin, Ena, used to stage entertainments in the hut. I gather they charged the local children a half-penny for the privilege of attending their performances.

The Kemp family was immense by modern standards and my mother had ten brothers and sisters. Several of my uncles were shipwrights in the Dockyard, one became steward of the golf course at Great Salterns, another was a senior employee of the Post Office. My impression was that he was Postmaster, since he worked in an office in the main post office. This was always an early visit when I came to Portsmouth as he invariably gave me half a crown which was five weeks pocket money to me and such wealth could only be appropriate to a postmaster.

From my earliest memories, we went to Portsmouth every summer for an extended stay with my aunt in Broad Street. I well remember the family chat about St. Thomas's Church being turned into a cathedral. The impression I got, at the age of about five, that it was a snobbish move and would put the church out of the reach of ordinary people. The fact that no one from the huge family, apart from the children in the choir, ever entered the church was irrelevant.

There were, and still are, a lot of pubs at the Point end of Broad Street. For some reason the Still and West was considered a sink of the greatest iniquity and from the phrase 'I saw him coming out of the Still and West' fixed the status of the drinker irrevocably. There was also a Gentlemens' Convenience on the Point which was completely masked by tin-plate advertisements for a cigarette called BDV. There were mysterious notices in the Gents warning the users against promiscuous sexual intercourse. Unlike my grandfather I was a very early reader but understanding lagged along way behind.

From the Point one could take either fork right or left. Both ways were of enormous interest. Taking the right hand, seaward side, one came into Bath Square where Uncle Alf (a Dockyard shipwright) and Aunty Letitia lived. Uncle Alf had a wireless set that would receive Radio Normandy when this station started and ensured my niche in Choral Society socials by enabling me to learn all the stirring advertising songs such as "Hurrah for Betox, what a delightful smell" and a song advertising horrible wheat flakes called 'Force' which assured us that 'Sunny Jim' leapt high o'er a fence to the tune of a French march 'La Reve Passee'.

The next point of interest on the seaward side (of West Street) was the Platform which we knew by the grand title of 'The Prom'. In fact it was a little railed off rectangle with rather rusty but imposing lanterns and railings. They must have rusted away by now. Alongside this was 'The Beach' which for years I thought was the archetypal of all beaches. It had some of the sharpest stones I have ever encountered. It was from this beach that the yachts and boats built by Harry Feltham were launched. His workshop was alongside 27 Broad Street and he built classic yachts which are now collectors pieces. He was a smallish bespectacled man who had little time for children, although he would always give us scraps of the beautiful wood he used. There were two Feltham brothers and George had one workshop further down Broad Street on the seaward side and another almost at the end of Broad Street on the Camber side. George had a son called Ron who took my elder sister yachting and in consequence I had the run of their sheds. They had a wonderful old gas engine to drive the overhead pulleys with an open crank and a 'hit and miss' governor. The governor controlled the speed of the engine by allowing it to fire when the speed needed to be beefed up and then shut off the gas allowing the engine to idle for a revolution or two. This formed a fascinating irregular rhythm which could well be utilised in modern music. There was a younger son of George called Roy. He built a 12 foot clinker dinghy when he was 14 and was featured on the children's page of the Daily Mirror below the adventures of 'Pip, Squeak and Wilfred'. It was part of the folklore that Harry and George Feltham were not on speaking terms. It was from the beach that we all learnt to swim. At low tide the older children would swim across the harbour entrance to Fort Blockhouse, a distance which in my childish memory seemed miles.

To the seaward side of the 'prom' were two impressive houses. One was owned by an artist called Wylie, while the other was the home of one of the Brickwood family, the famous Portsmouth brewers. Still further on was the boomyard where the massive windlasses used to stream the beam across the harbour mouth during the 14-18 war lay in considerable disarray. It was protected by a gate with a huge padlock. The protection offered no problems to a small boy and I spent many happy hours examining the machinery imagining how it might work. There were few who abandoned it in 1918 who could have imagined it would be in use again 21 years after.

There were always interesting craft at the quay including private yachts and on one occasion a London 'Spritty' barge which was sailed single handed by an ancient man called Bob. I think he sometimes had a boy to help but considering it was some 80 feet long it was quite a remarkable feet.

I now realise how much of my future life was moulded by my early visits to Point. I saw the Howe, Rodney, Nelson and Queen Elizabeth pass by the 'prom' and wondered at the immensity of these giants which were, had we realised it, been obsolete since the end of the Great War. It was only a short walk to the sea front near Clarence Pier where I watched the sea planes of the Schneider Trophy race, little imagining that I was witnessing the testing of the predecessor of the Spitfire which played such a great part in winning the Battle of Britain.

Old Portsmouth was Broad Street to an old Pointer. When one went as far as the High Street you were on alien territory, unless it was to visit the superb fish and chip shop there for a penny fish and a ha'peth of chips. Apart from this there was nothing which couldn't be found in Broad Street and the quay. Being incurably sentimental I sometimes believe that all 'Old Pointers' finally shuffle off this mortal coil to the salute of the 'nine o'clock gun' which resounded over Portsmouth every day and provided the few Pointers who possessed watches with a forerunner of the Greenwich time signal."

Roy Williams

"I am going to tell you about a few memories of the time I spent in Old Portsmouth. I had rented at 7/6d a week a little flat in Penny Street, which was over the garage that was the back way of the Provost of Portsmouth's large and lovely house. The front of it facing what I think was called Pembroke Gardens.

Penny Street was little terraced houses opposite a Naval Officers' Club. From the bedroom window you could see the Garrison Church, the old brewery and the round tower.

Let me tell you a story about the old brewery. My husband, who was on leave from the Navy and I went to bed. In the middle of the night our baby son woke up crying, so I got up to calm him down, when all of a sudden, I woke my husband up, as I thought that something was going on outside as there was a lot of noise. We both opened the window quietly and there were three men with torches, loading up a big van with what I think were crates of wines and spirits, etc. We watched for a few minutes, then closed the window, in case they saw us. There was no way I could warn anyone as there was no phone box near us and we were frightened. The next day two men knocked on our little front door and said they were police, which I had already gathered because of the way they spoke. They asked us if we had heard any noise, etc. So my husband and I told them what we had seen and heard. We never heard what happened after that, but the evening papers said that there had been a burglary there.

Well, the following week, we had another surprise. There seemed to be a lot of people out in the street, and we could see from our window that a ship had gone aground, I think it was HMS Nelson.

I often pushed my baby around by the Clarence Barracks to let him watch the soldiers doing their training.

When my husband was on leave we used to go down to Sallyport and catch fish, the water always seemed warm there.

I hope someone who reads my little story will remember some of what I have written."

Mrs K. E. Smith

"In the early twenties before I had left school one of my family duties (which were shared with two of my sisters) was to make sure that my father got a hot dinner. This was not as straight forward as it sounds. You see, the family home was in Copnor and my father was in Old Portsmouth.

The usual routine was as follows. First of all this duty had to be accomplished in the school dinner break which I think was 1½ hours. My sisters and I came out of Copnor Road school together but endeavoured to lose each other before we got home to Highgate Road. The reason being that the first home had to do the trip. (In fairness to my mum I think we all did our fair share regardless) If it was my turn then I would pick up the hot dinner which would be on a plate, wrapped in a tea towel and finally wrapped in plenty of brown paper to keep it warm. I would then have to run to catch the tram at Copnor Bridge. Running in heeled lace up boots and a long skirt whilst carrying was not easy and I dared not spill any and as for dropping it and breaking the plates well....!

The tram went up New Road, into Lake Road, Commercial Road, Guildhall and then down the High Street to Broad Street where I got off at the end of the journey. The place where my father, Frank Jafkins, worked was Timothy Whites warehouse in Broad Street where at this time he was the relief manager. The entrance was a small black door at the top of two steps set in a brick wall with some windows. The building was not very big but was absolutely full of stock as it was the supplier to all the local Timothy White branches. The thing I remember was the smell, with quantities of stuff like paraffin in bulk, methylated spirits, starch, soda, candles & firewood the odour given off was anything but pleasant. As well as these everything else that was sold by the shops was kept here. From matches to paraffin stoves, stacks of soap, Sunlight, Lifebuoy, Carbolic and others. Soap was used for washing everything in those days. If you were unfortunate to pick up the soap after it had been used for something else and had particles of grit embedded in it and then proceeded to use it on some delicate part of your anatomy, you soon knew all about it! The firewood sold for a ½d a bundle, loose starch 2d a pound, loose soda 1d a pound. The meths then was colourless but because some unfortunate drunk the stuff, even then, the authorities decided if it was coloured purple it would put them off. Wrong again! The building was gas lit and with the windows in the front was not too dark but I always imagined that the corners behind all the piles of stuff hid rats but I never saw any. My father was scrupulously honest and always insisted on my mother paying him first before he would bring any supplies home that she wanted. Other local people would also come into the warehouse to buy items which left my father with cash but nowhere to keep it. He solved this problem by getting a blue canvas bag into which the money went and the lot buried every night for a week, until it was banked on Fridays, in the bottom of the large soda drum and the lid replaced. Not very secure but it worked.

After giving Dad his dinner it was a rush to catch a tram back home and only then could I have my own dinner. If the trams were late then it was grab what I could and eat it while running back to school. All of this only took place if Mum could afford the tram fare and at the best was only about three times a week. If there was no money or if the weather was bad well, I suppose Dad had sandwiches."

Mrs E.M.Garlick

"A regular Sunday morning treat was to accompany the soldiers from Victoria Barracks and Clarence Barracks going to Church Parade at the Garrison Church on Governor's Green in Penny Street. While they were attending morning service we would visit Sally Port or the Camber Docks and be back in time for the bugler calling the markers to fall in. As the brass bands and marching platoons moved off we would march along with them back to their barracks. Sometimes the band would play on the lawns in front of the Officers' Mess and the public would be allowed into the barracks to watch and listen to selections of popular music. I recall several regiments including the South Wales Borderers which had a large white goat as a Regimental Mascot. Also, the King's Own Scottish Borderers were stationed there for some time and I remember experiencing a mild disappointment that while the pipers wore kilts other soldiers wore tartan trousers.

Things may be very different now but when I was leaving school the tradition was for sons to go and work where their fathers were employed. My father, grand-father and great-grandfather, I knew had all been shipyard workers and it seemed quite logical that I should continue the sequence. At the school handicraft centre - 'manual', as it was known to us, I had shown an aptitude for woodwork and thought this might be the best pursuit for me to follow. My father, knowing of my interest in woodwork, asked me if I wanted to be a joiner or a boat-builder so that he could make the appropriate application for my apprenticeship at Vospers. I give a wry grin now as I consider how my whole life has been conditioned by the answer that I gave to that simple question, and of the doubtful logic upon which my choice was based. I asked my father about what my choice would entail, to which he replied that either I would work under Mr. Cox, who ran the joiners' shop, or Mr. Staples, who was the Chargeman of the boat-shop. Mr. Cox was an elderly, rather irascible gentleman with a pronounced red nose, so I did not fancy working for him. Mr. Staples, whose son and I had been playmates had once given me tuppence for making a rather spectacular catch and bowled dismissal of him when we played cricket on Pembroke Gardens. I elected, therefore, to become a boat-builder apprentice without really appreciating what it was all about. I must say that I never regretted my haphazard choice for I enjoyed the work and it led, ultimately to my career as a naval shipwright. I still recall my first morning in boat-shop and how in my earnest endeavour to make a good impression I worked very rapidly, if somewhat inexpertly. My instructor was a kindly, retired Dockyard Shipwright called Charlie Ward who, as we stopped work when the hooter blew at 12 o'clock, said "You'll learn, my son, you'll learn". I did, in fact, learn many things from that benign old gentleman, particularly skills of the trade which left me with a craftsman's eye and a love of wood which still persists. Charlie told me of a remarkable coincidence, namely that he, who was my first trade instructor, had been put to work under my grandfather, also a shipwright, when he first went to work in Portsmouth Dockyard in the 1890s. Such is the long-arm of coincidence and I would like to think that some of our family traditions were passed on by this rather devious route.

The work was quite hard, occasionally a bit repetitive and, in my view, distinctly under-paid. During 1938 and 1939, I received five shillings only a week, less 4d for National Insurance Stamps. I recognise that these wages were standard rates for all young apprentices but after giving half to my parents towards my keep, the remainder seemed scant reward for 47 hours of fairly hard work. So I soon learned from other lads a way of augmenting my pocket money. The men in the boat-shops and shipyard, used to like a snack in the mornings - there was a 15 minute break at 10am - and those who had not brought any food used to send we lads out to nearby cafes or cook-shops to purchase cheese-rolls, meat-rolls or cakes for them. Leaving the premises was not really allowed so we had to climb over the back-gate into White Hart Road to get to Whymarks in Oyster Street, or somewhere similar, to purchase the snacks. These used to cost 2d or 3d each and if there was 1d or 2d change we were usually given for running this errand. Not always, I hasten to add, for some men thought it was part of our duties to go out for them. Funny, how quickly I learned who would be likely to give a tip and how to avoid those who would not!

In my early days at Vospers I took my share of the leg-pulling which is the inevitable experience of the novice, especially if, like me, you have ginger hair and a rather trusting nature. In the first week or so, I was sent to the Boiler shop to ask Mr. Penfold for a 'long stand'. Thinking this might be some sort of supporting trestle needed for our current operation, I did as instructed. After waiting a couple of minutes I sensed something was amiss which contributed to the amusement of a group of platers, nearby. So I swallowed my embarrassment and returned to shipyard, chastened, annoyed and vowing never to get caught out like that again. Some time later, the Chargeman called me over and instructed me to go to the Loan Tool Store and fetch him a 'long level'. Sensing that I was being set-up again, I did not go to the store but returned and said that the 'long level' was unavailable. Almost immediately afterwards, Mr. Staples went to the store himself and returned with the four foot long spirit level. Once again I was somewhat chastened and annoyed - at my naivety. But I quickly learned the difference between a proper order and a prank and before long I was subjecting later arrivals to similar leg-pulls.

R.C.Daniels

Schooling

"The day after our arrival in High Street I started attending Portsmouth Town School, a 3-storey red brick Victorian building adjacent to the power station in Gunwharf Road. Its appearance was marred by a coating of coal-dust from the stockpiles of furnace fuel alongside the Camber dock on the opposite side of the road. It was probably one of the oldest council schools in Portsmouth built just a few yards from its historic predecessor, the little house-cum-workshop in Highbury Street where John Pounds once ran his famous school for ragged children. By comparison the Town School was a fine building with high gables over the top-storey windows. Infant scholars used the ground floor, Junior Girls on the first floor and we Junior Boys were located on the top floor. There was no mixing of these groups - coeducation stopped at seven years and there were designated stairways to each floor, except for the external iron fire-escapes. There was gas lighting and coal fires. The cloakrooms were inside the building but not the toilets - not for boys, anyway. To the rear were to asphalt surfaced playgrounds with a separating wall and a small wicker-gate. Pupils passed through this gate only when instructed by the staff for mixing of the sexes was taboo! A corrugated-iron roofed area was immediately adjacent to the building though this was barely capable of accommodating the assembled classes when it was raining. We played with our neighbourhood pals at playtime but were allocated to houses for P.T. and other recreational activities.

Our form master, Mr. G.P. Clarke was a keen cricket enthusiast who endeavoured to instil the art of keeping square bat and reaching forward to the ball. I recall he enlisted the ready assistance of Mr. Spicer, a local newsagent in Highbury Street, to impart the finer points of the willow wand. There were few items in the cricket-bag available for playground coaching yet we all wanted to hold the one or two cricket bats available, being disappointed if all we could get was a stump to practise with. Mr. Clarke was the Senior Master but the Head was Mr. A. J. Smith, an elderly, autocratic gentleman with a high stiff collar which did not hide the loose skin at his throat. Hence his derogatory nickname of "crabneck". He was a quiet man, strict but fair and perhaps the cannings he inflicted hurt him more than the recipients. Our Mr. Clarke, who went on to live to a ripe and active old age, seemed to me to be much more affable though, of course, like all school-teachers of those times he was a strict disciplinarian. He had a permanent black spot on the tip of his nose which playground rumour held as being caused by some recalcitrant pupil throwing a school-pen at his face during a classroom altercation.

Teaching the three R's was the mode of instruction then and I have no recollection of it being the boring chore that latter-day educationalists would have us believe. We learned by rote; multiplication tables, simple formulae, songs and poems, most of which I can recite after 50 odd years. There was morning assembly with prayers and a hymn but no particular emphasis on Religious Instruction. A rather attractive lady teacher, Miss. Cunliffe, played the piano at Assembly and taught us to have a basic appreciation of music. She also ran a school play that year - a comedy in which I played a haughty butler. Being rather shy and not too good at remembering my lines, I was not a great success although I did add, unconsciously to the comedy.

I remember the French onion boats and Jersey potato barges which came to the Camber each summer in the thirties. A French lad, I believe his name was Paul, accompanied his family and lived in their warehouse in Oyster Street. He used to attend our school, whether to satisfy the law or improve his English, I am not sure. The French onion men used to ride around the town on bicycles selling strings of excellent onions which they carried on a broomstick over their shoulder. In the evenings they sat on the quay-side drinking red wine and singing strange songs to the distinctive sounds of their French concertinas and accordions.

I was at the Town School for one year only for in 1935 not only had I now reached senior school age but the school was to be demolished.

ONION MAN

I and a classmate called Tom Jefferies, who lived in Highbury Street, were tasked with sketching our old school, allegedly to be placed in the Cumberland House Museum. Tom and I perched on the rear entrance gateposts and sketched the east elevation of the building. I had scant understanding of things like perspective and tried to include far too much detail of the brickwork. Hence my sketch was not very good and I still remember my disappointment with my efforts. I wish I had been able to leave something more worthwhile to perpetuate the memory of some really happy days at Portsmouth Town, unfortunately what I produced would not have earned a place on the classroom wall."

R. C. Daniels

Electricity

"The electricity for the City of Portsmouth was provided by the power station in Old Portsmouth. A private company originally sought permission to supply electricity to the then Borough of Portsmouth. However, the council decided to apply for an order themselves. This was granted in 1890 and in 1892 the building of the power station in Highbury Street commenced. The supply was inaugurated in June 1894, with about 70 consumers. Portsmouth was unusual in that AC supply by Ferranti was used from the outset.

The station had its own dock at the camber where the colliers from Tyneside could berth and discharge at all states of the tide. In 1935/6 the station was extended with additional generating plant and ancillary plant. The first of two new 30,000 kilowatt generators was put on load on the 4th of August 1938. Exactly three weeks later this machine was completely wrecked in an explosion, causing considerable damage to the building and large portions of the machine were thrown through the roof into the harbour and foreshore.

The machine was replaced only to be destroyed a few years later in the blitz."

The Evening News carried a report on the 1938 incident. "A piece of metal weighing one and a half hundredweight hurtled over Old

Portsmouth last night and landed on the beach at Point, as a result of an explosion at the new premises of the City Electricity Undertaking in Gunwharf Road......The explosion occurred just before 6.30pm in the new turbo-alternator, started only three weeks ago by the Lady Mayoress of Portsmouth, and not yet handed over to the company by the manufacturers.....Windows were smashed in the vicinity and people for a long way round felt the shock of the explosion.....Those nearest to the place where the metal fell were Mr Frank Butcher, a local waterman, and his brother, who were on the slipway at the time, while their two nephews were on the beach not far away."

The Hospital

"It was in 1925 at the age of 17 years that my local doctor by the name of Lewis, sent me to the Eye and Ear Hospital in Pembroke Road. Despite the title of the hospital, I was sent there for treatment to my nostrils.

When I arrived, having made my own way there from my home in Jersey Road, Buckland. (No ambulance service then) I found my way into a fairly large room which served as the waiting room. I seem to remember the walls being washed over with a pale green paint with the standard wooden rubbing strip about three feet from the floor.

The hospital served the outlying districts as well as Portsmouth proper. This resulted in the organising body of the hospital making a very rigid ruling that anybody from outside the Portsmouth boundaries would be dealt with first. Consequently it was not necessarily first come - first served. Eventually a nurse called my name and directed me down the corridor to the surgery where I was greeted and examined by Dr Scott-Reidout, reputedly a Harley Street specialist. He had with him a trainee who I presume hoped to emulate the great man in years to come.

It was decided that I should be admitted for treatment so about four weeks later I made by way back to be admitted to an all male ward on the first floor. This contained nine beds. Came the operation, no pre-med in those days, just chloroformed pad over the face and away you went. When I came to there was the hospital porter bending over me saying "If you want to take it out on somebody, take it out on me, not the matron." I presumed that the after effects of the chloroform made some people violent.

The staff consisted of Matron Clay, who was the traditional matron, a right tartar; a sister, quite the opposite, several nurses and the male porter. I don't remember much about the wards but the beds were the old steel frame type and the lighting was electric. The food was plain but good and there were three meals a day.

I was there for about two and a half weeks, longer than anticipated as the bleeding from my nose would not stop but as I progressed I was allowed to relieve the boredom by taking flowers from the ward to the kitchen each night, (this was to preserve the oxygen in the ward) trim them and put them in fresh water ready to be taken back to the wards the next morning.

As you got fitter sister or matron pronounced whether you were allowed out and I took advantage of this whenever possible. It was nice to get some exercise after being cooped up indoors. Whilst it was a good view across Governor's Green from the day room (also on the first floor) it was better to stroll across in person. There appeared to be no Sunday Parades by the military while I was there. I remember my father taking me down to see them when I was younger but I don't know if they were revived after the Great War.

Traffic was practically non-existent so it was a peaceful interlude for me. Not all that enjoyable but I never did find out what they actually did to me."

H. S. J. (Bert) Garlick

The Camber

"My memories of Spice Island pivot around the thirties, when I was a lad. In the summer I would take my fishing tackle, a bottle of cold tea and a few jam butties and try my luck in the camber. It usually turned out to be a feeding session for the fishes, I think they liked my particular bait of rag worm, for I landed nothing more exciting than a dogfish. When my supply of bait ran out I would stroll around the camber to see how the other boys had fared with their fishing. Their luck was not much better than mine. On my return home mother would ask what I had brought home for tea? I'd say "I guess they weren't biting today" and was sent over the fish shop to get 3 tuppennies and three penn'eth of chips.

TYPICAL CAMBER SCENE

Victoria Pier made a nice change of venue for fishing but it still brought me the same result. I amused myself pitching pebbles into the sea and making them bounce across the water. I liked watching the various crafts entering and leaving harbour. If I saw a warship pass by it made my day.

Another memory I have is of the French 'Johnnie Onion' men taking their stock of onions from the boat at the Camber to their lock-up in White Hart Lane where they weaved and spliced them together to hang on the handle bars of their cycles, before selling them to the housewives of Portsmouth and beyond. Pieces of plywood prevented the strings of onions fouling the spokes of the wheels."

F. Ford

"When school-time was over, playtime began and in Old Portsmouth there was much to explore and many things to do. In those days, despite being one of the less salubrious areas of Portsmouth, here was a place where children could roam the streets and open places in relative safety. The Camber was an inviting, if hazardous, playground where we used to go swimming in the cooling-water discharge from the nearby power-station. We called it the 'Bunny', I never established why. We used to dive into the rushing torrent of lukewarm water emerging from the large pipes to be carried swiftly to the other side of the Camber. Apart from the warmth of the water, I found swimming around the Bunny less inviting than swimming off the beaches. It was nowhere near as refreshing or exhilarating. The warmer water was, however, attractive to the shoals of sea-bass and mullet which swarmed in this area of the Camber. Anglers would sit watching their floats bobbing up and down for hours in the evenings when the fish seemed to be attracted to the light of the quay-side lamps. This sport was popular but personally, I found it tedious, for I lacked both the necessary patience - and suitable fishing tackle!

Sometimes, when local fisherman had secured their boats for the night, we would 'borrow' one of their small dinghies or rowing-boats and paddle it around the Camber moorings. Occasionally, we would be fortunate enough to find an oar left in the bilges of the boat which would enable us to scull over the stern, but more often than not we had to use a floor-board to propel the boat through the water. We were always careful to re-secure the boat to a ladder or mooring ring with sufficient slack on the painter to allow for the rise and fall of the tide. I suppose that such 'borrowings' would be less sympathctically accepted by boat-owners and fisherman, today. Perhaps it was because we were more careful for I cannot recall these boats ever getting damaged. I do, however, remember one occasion when several of us were stranded on a mud-flat as the tide went out. This was the sort of thing we usually took great pains to avoid. It caused me to do some frantic thinking on my way home where I arrived two hours late and had to invent some lame excuse about being at a friend's house and not noticing the clock had stopped.

One spot which held a particular attraction and was often visited was the Hot Walls, or Boy's Beach as we called it. Here we ambled along the waters edge, preferably soon after the tide had receded. We would search for crabs beneath the rocks, occasionally finding a sand-eel or baby dog-fish as we wandered along the beach as far as Clarence Pier. The pier's supporting piles were surrounded by metal bars to prevent people getting beneath the landing-jetty, but we boys found a gap where we would climb up and squeeze through the bars to look for pennies dropped from the fun-fair above. I cannot remember finding any, but I do recall one exceptionally low ebb-tide receding far enough to leave the shore on the seaward side of the pier exposed for a short while. Not many people can claim to have walked on the south side of Clarence Pier!

In 1938 (or perhaps it was 1939) with a girl-friend and two other lads I swam over to the Gosport side from just below Round Tower. The quarter of a mile, or so, each way was not particularly demanding but to the uninitiated it could be quite hazardous, for even at slack water we were aware of currents running in opposite directions as we made our return journey. When part-way back we saw an Isle of Wight paddle-steamer leaving Harbour Station jetty, this caused what I now recognise as an adrenalin-boost which enabled us to reach the Pompey side in extra-quick time. Later, in 1940 when all other beaches in Portsmouth were closed we used to swim off Pickford's Beach and got used to the strong currents running in the harbour mouth."

R. C. Daniels

This booklet was compiled by the members of the W.E.A. Local History Group which meets at the New Road Adult Education Centre, Balliol Road, Buckland. The group is made up of local people who wish to record the history of ordinary peoples' lives and the streets in which they live. The group is very informal and welcomes new members who care to come to New Road on a Tuesday evening during term time or write to us.

Class Members:

Leonard Bufton, Anton Cox, Sandy Ellerton, Frank Ford (Sketches), Betty Fowkes, Peter Galvin, Malcolm Garlick (Sketches), Charles Hutchins, Brian Knight, George Linton, Stephen Pomeroy (Editor), Gina Priseman, Jeff Smith, Don Tallack, Rita Wall and Margaret Webster.

Contributors:

R. C. Daniels, Mrs E. M. Garlick, H. S. J. Garlick,
Mrs K. E. Smith, Mr M. A. Tucker, Roy Williams.

Honorary Members:

Don Miles (Typesetting), Edward Pomeroy (Proof reader).

Affiliated Members:

Des Beaumont, Morecambe, Lancashire

Vic Burly, Brisbane, Australia

Maggie Munro, Frankstone, Australia

Second Printing : 1997

WEA (Portsmouth Branch Local History Group)
Adult Education Centre
New Road
Buckland

ISBN 1 873911 02 5

Typeset and Printed in England
by
Printcraft, 108 Marmion Road, Southsea, Hampshire PO5 2BB